WRITER'S LITTLE BOOK OF WISDOM

A treasury of tips and warnings for every writer and aspiring writer--the traps to avoid and gold mines to explore.

By John Long

ICS BOOKS, Inc.

ICS BOOKS, Inc.
Merrillville, IN

Writer's Little Book of Wisdom

Copyright © 1996 by John Long   Cover photo: Walter Gray Photography

10 9 8 7 6 5 4 3 2 1

Published by:
ICS BOOKS, Inc
1370 E. 86th Place
Merrillville, IN 46410
800-541-7323

Co-Published in Canada by:
Vanwell Publishing LTD
1 Northrup Crescent
St. Catharines, Ontario
L2M 6P5
800-661-6136

Printed in the U.S.A.
All ICS titles are printed on 50% recycled paper from
pre-consumer waste. All sheets are processed without
using acid.

Library of Congress Cataloging-in-Publication Data

Long, John
    Writer's little book of wisdom / by John Long.
        p. cm.
    ISBN 1-57034-037-4
    1. Authorship - - Humor. I. Title.
PN169 . L66   1996
808' . 02'0207--dc20   96-1294
                                        CIP

Dedication

To my wife, Mariana Rondon-Mendez, who through all stormy weather has never abandoned ship.

Credits.

Thanks to my editor, Gail Bradney, my agent, Bernard Shir-Cliff, ICS publisher, Tom Todd, and fellow confidant and fellow, writer, Paul Edwards, who all scoured this little book and made valuable suggestions.

Introduction

On the long road toward mastery, the first mile has little to do with high art, and much to do with basic composition, narrative technique and story architecture. Once that first mile is past, rules, formulas and the wisdom of every gifted writer who ever lived are of limited value. Every writer must find his own way, stumbling past the threshold of feelings, into which all great writing must go. Themes can lead us to the feelings, and help keep us there; and technique can give us a voice as we make our way through our own basic stuff. But neither can replace the introspection crucial to serious writing.

Throughout this little book my aim has been to point out both common failures and gold mines, and the straightest paths that I know of to the latter. Many writers have wasted half their professional lives following bogus procedures and working from foggy assumptions. In trying to address these things I often lacked space to adequately explain the why of it all. But providing a writer is exposed to the long road, and knows some practical guidelines about driving, he is bound to arrive somewhere authenticgiven the knack and the willingness to work hard.

1.   Art without practice is nothing.

2.   Sit down every day and write.

3.   Of the writers I know who own
       mansions, all of them could paper the
       outside of their house with rejection
       notices.

4.   The blank page or empty screen is
       agonizing to fill and always will be.

5.   Unless you approach writing as a discipline, and not a task, you'll never see the rainbow for the rain.

6. "I get up in the morning, go into the office and tie myself into the chair with the sash of my bathrobe."
   -John McPhee

7. The habit of work unlocks the vault marked "talent."

8. When an idea seems especially luminous, never let the fear of failure keep you from trying to capture it in words.

9.   Sometimes I must coax out the words; other times I must haul them out, but I can never beg or my command is lost.

10.   When writing becomes torturous, you're trying too hard.

11.   The value of a staff job is that you must produce.

12.   Turn over parts of yourself
that scream to be left alone.

13. Lose the aspect of self-examination and writing is never more than craft.

14. Self examination is painful but liberating.

15. Self indulgence feels plausible but imprisons.

16. Self examination is brutally honest. Self indulgence is brutally maudlin.

17. Self examination sheds light. Self indulgence absorbs it.

18. Self examination can dredge up universal truths.

19. The mumblings of self indulgence interest only sycophants and conscience-stricken mothers.

20. The best medicine for lack of discipline is an assignment, a deadline and a stack of bills.

21. There is no single technique to unlock your words, save sitting down and writing.

22. Faulkner said, "The tools I need for work are paper, tobacco, food and a little whisky."

23. Some writers can't work without a dalmatian, a log cabin, the London Philharmonic Orchestra. Whatever works...

24. Most writers have a gift for some, or even several, aspects of the craft, but no one is a natural at the whole process.

25. Georges Simenon, Dickens, Trollope, Balzac, Thomas Wolfe, Victor Hugo—each turned out millions of words a year, so it can be done.

26. "Thinking about it" is a superb way to stay on your ass and avoid writing.

27. Expect, allow and accept that every first draft will represent your lowest standard. And have at it.

28. First priority: Get that first draft cranked out.

29. Ground breaking work sometimes comes when you least feel like writing.

30. Take a break. Work your body. (Hate sports? Take a walk.)

31. People who complain that writing is desperate "work" have never dug a trench under gunfire or tried to cut away a malfunctioning parachute.

32. Red Smith claimed writing was easy. "All you do is sit down at a typewriter and open a vein."

33. Jot down the signposts, then later go back and sketch in the terrain.

34. Great writing is a mode of transportation.

35. Take monumental risks.

36. Wrestle your worst fear, expose your greatest anger and deepest passion.

37. A story that doesn't challenge the writer won't challenge the reader either.

38. Every writer must discover his OCL (optimum caffeine level).

39. Too little coffee and you spend the morning watering the ferns; too much and you'll need to pick a fight with a Navy SEAL.

40. Like the Turks say, coffee should be black as hell and strong as death.

41. Add sugar only at the risk of writing Harlequin romances.

42. Writer's block often results from beating your brains out trying to punch a hole through a dead end.

43. Techniques for breaking blocks include: spontaneously writing in a journal; talking into a tape recorder and playing it back; screaming, chopping wood, throwing heavy objects.

44. No block can be overcome by hard liquor, fretting or self-beating. You might have to go all the way down before you can effect any upward movement.

45.   A word is a blunt nail or a loose net to secure an idea.

46.   As the writer's tools, words are hopelessly inadequate.

47.   The more profound the idea or feeling, the more lacking are the tools for the task.

48. Most bad styles result from poor word choice.

49. You can find the right word(s) only when you know exactly how you feel.

50. Using another writer's words is like wearing someone else's shoes: they'll never fit because they've been broken in on someone else's feet.

51. If you have to look a word up, don't use it.

52. Clowning with words and jargon pollutes a pure style, but totally avoiding whimsy can flatten a potential masterpiece.

53. Avoid amazingly agile alliterations. Avoid foreign words where there is a perfectly good English equivalent.

54. The urge to decorate descriptions comes from the allure of using words for their own sake.

55. Persuasive words are never brooded over and merely selected, they are torn from our guts.

56. "Very" is very often used to amplify very pedestrian statements.

57. No bureaucratese ("accessing the infrastructure").

58.   In expository prose, dump all qualifiers: rather, little, pretty, et al.

59.   In dialogue, however, it sounds unnatural not to use qualifiers, since everyone uses them in normal conversation.

60.   Avoid substituting adjectives and adverbs for vivid nouns and verbs.

61. To write intuitively involves
     many mysterious factors, but
     present is a bone-deep feel
     for the inner nature of things.

62. The slippery part of trying to seize insight with words is that unlike thought, words and feelings are unrelated.

63. Concrete words engage the five senses.

64. Unless meaning and value are somehow implied, all the concrete details in the world leave one unmoved.

65. Draw attention to the words and the reader squirms.

66.   Focus on the thoughts and the reader tires.

67.   Muster up the feelings and the reader lives two lives at once: his own, and the one he's reading.

68. In *The Art of Fiction*, John Gardner warns against filtering an image through some observing consciousness: "Turning, she noticed two snakes fighting among the rocks," should be replaced with, "She turned. In among the rocks, two snakes were fighting."

69.   Meaning is dignified by words, but in and of themselves, words have no meaning.

70.   Too many words clog the action and blunt the dramatic saber.

71.   The relevancy of a word is not its history, but its face value in current usage.

72. "Five-dollar words usually overstate the thing, throwing doubt on your judgment and poise."

    – E.B. White

73. Fluid, easy wording keeps attention on the story, not the writing.

74. The adjective is the banana peel on the writer's study floor.

75.   Words. Ten thousand words. How do I
      pick the right ones? It often seems the
      best words pick me. They float up from
      emptiness and land on whatever I'm
      thinking or feeling.

76.   Conjunctions provide liquid transitions
      between images, feelings and ideas.

77.   A long sentence can rarely relate its
      sense unless it's simply constructed.

78. Short sentences convey pace, and are the rails of action writing; longer sentences feel more formal and deliberate, and are typically better suited for exposition.

79. William Strunk Jr. said that "Vigorous writing is concise. A sentence should contain no unnecessary words for the same reason that a machine should have no unnecessary parts."

80. Strength and vividness leap off direct statements.

81. Use the positive form: "He was not very often well-clad," should be, "He dressed like a bum."

82. Emphasis is secured by the position of the key word(s).

83. "For wanton jerks, my husband stands head of the class." This emphasizes the husband's character more effectively than, "My husband stands head of the class of wanton jerks."

84.　Contrast opposites by containing them within a single sentence. "He motored to Vegas in a Coupe de Ville, and he walked back home in a barrel."

85.　A paragraph indentation cues the reader to pause and take a deep breath.

86. The first sentence of a paragraph typically suggests the topic or helps the transition from the previous paragraph.

87. Rarely can you fully develope an idea or feeling in one paragraph.

88. Never insist that a paragraph cultivates more than a point or facet of an idea or feeling.

89. Overdeveloping a thought or feeling in one paragraph can produce writing so dense a reader needs a machete to get through it.

90. The paragraph is a lump of clay that takes its shape from the thought or feeling it has to express.

91. In the hands of an artist, the shape of a paragraph *is* the thought or feeling.

92. Every paragraph should project a roundness, a sense that the images, thoughts and feelings contained form a unit unto themselves.

93. Breaking up overloaded paragraphs normally improves them.

94. When the pulse is not carried over from one sentence to the next, the timing feels uneven and the sentences don't seem to belong to each other.

95. "The sentences in a paragraph have the same connection with each other that marbles have with a bag: they touch without adhering."
    – *Coleridge*

96. There is no "right" length for a paragraph, but a reader is daunted by a solid page of text.

97. Hone your craft by picking apart and analyzing a few paragraphs of a writer you admire.

98.   Use repetition for emphasis, humor, irony. "Brutus is an honorable man. They are all honorable men."

99.   Punctuation should be as invisible as brush strokes on a watercolor.

100. Every punctuation mark represents a unit of pause. Avoid damming the narrative stream.

101. Dump any comma, semicolon, colon or dash that does not help clarify sense and meaning.

102. Copy editors punctuate according to rules. But clarity of meaning, not style-manual "correctness," is the best criterion.

103. Drop ornate punctuation and work toward simplicity.

104. Whatever is read is silently spoken and naturally punctuated when we breathe.

105. A chapter break resembles the landing in a long flight of stairs. It offers the reader a place to rest and ponder the height gained, the climb ahead.

106. Epithets should always aim at vividness.

107. Freighting a sentence with epithets is the business of obituary columnists and greeting card writers.

108.   Use only those epithets that further action, interest or meaning.

109.   Epithets work best when the expression demands one epithet and no other: "The corpse was frozen stiff."

110. "We veered round a glistening minaret of blue ice, rearing from the deep like frozen doom," is an example of an author trying too hard. "Ice, mast high, floated by," shows that a writer is better off letting the image, rather than the words, do the work.

111. Decorative metaphors sometimes enliven poetry and always murder prose.

112. Metaphors have little place in narrative prose, only in exposition, and rarely then. Useful metaphors illuminate an equivalence.

113. Strong metaphors clarify meaning by dilating our imaginations.

114. "Shotgun" (i.e., forced, as in "shotgun wedding") metaphors try to marry a king snake and a porcupine.

115. Jonathan Swift, an exceptional stylist by any measure, rarely used metaphors.

116. Point of view, or "person," must be decided before you write a single line.

117. The omniscient third-person narrator knows the characters better than they know themselves.

118. The limited omniscient viewpoint is the voice of the twentieth century.

119. Limited omniscient voicing lets the reader join the character in an odyssey of discovery.

120. Inexperienced writers often write in first person.

121. If a story isn't working in the first person, try changing the point of view to the third person.

122. Changing point of view creates a totally different story, and often broadens the scope.

123. Flashbacks are useful to clarify and flesh out the plot, which unfolds in the present tense.

124. Most flashbacks come early on in the story, illuminating a character or event in light of things past.

125. Be aware of "front-loading" a story with flashbacks. Better to space them throughout. Sparingly.

126. A flashback is usually preferable to having a character (in dialogue) or narrator "explain" the back story.

127. Effective flashbacks are all about timing.

128. A character without a purpose is a story without a cause.

129. Give a character a valid grievance.

130. The fact that one character wants to explore Saturn and another character wants to elope with the janitor's stepdaughter is of little importance. It's the intensity of the wanting that fuels the story.

131. Know what a character wants, generically and specifically, even if the character does not.

132. Work to make a character achieve a credible degree of salvation in an unresolved world.

133. Feelings should vibrate from what a character does, how he moves and what he says.

134. Sensual and emotional vividness give us a sense of who a character is.

135. A character without inner turmoil or contradictions belongs in vestments or in a coffin, not in a story.

136. An active voice brings characters to life: "She slapped the deacon in the face."

137. Characters who lack a coarse streak usually have a mean one.

138. A character faces a crisis. He must change, or die. Desperate, he takes action. Fill in the blanks.

139. Most people cannot and will not change unless financial, physical, emotional and spiritual ruin forces them to.

140. If your character isn't a melange of your father, boss, childhood bully, neighbor, and the corner tamale vendor, chances are you've created a cartoon.

141. Allow characters to reveal themselves through words, thoughts and deeds.

142. Never announce character traits to the reader.

143. Memorable characters do normal things in unforgettable ways.

144. Characters who do unbelievable things are often unbelievable.

145. Words and behavior match only in the most exceptional people.

146. It is uncanny that the degree to which we feel for a character is relative to how much that character changes in the course of the tale.

147. A character might lie, but his body
      rarely does.

148. Tone and body language are the internal
      externalized.

149. Male writers will always stumble over female characters if they approach them as women first and human beings second.

150. There is only one thing more important than a character's actions: what he thinks about before he goes to sleep.

151. You must master dialogue. Period.

152. Dialogue is disrespected by those who cannot write it.

153. Dialogue writing is made easier if you understand that most people are poor listeners.

154. Nothing has trashed the art of dialogue writing more than television, with its daffy question-answer exchanges.

155. In authentic conversation a direct question is rarely asked, and a straight answer almost never given.

156. When a "point" is made in real conversation, it's brokered through countless interruptions, people talking over each other, snorting, sighing, hand waving, breaking wind and so forth.

157. Wooden dialogue comes from someone thinking out loud rather than feeling out loud.

158. Like fuel, dialogue should never be wasted.

159. Skillful dialogue is so individual and appropriate to each character that readers should know who's speaking without the attribution.

160. If dialogue doesn't reveal new information about character or atmosphere, axe it.

161. When a character's dialogue eludes you, write two monologues in the character's own words, starting with: "This is how I feel," and "This is what I think" about the given situation.

162. Crack dialogue alters the relationship between characters.

163. Look to old movies ('40s and '50s) for classic dialogue.

164. If you have an area of expertise, use it.

165. The qualitative feel of a scene is enhanced by appropriate rhythm and tone, and diminished by deluxe wording.

166. Avoid details that sound and feel like stage properties.

167. Grab and hold a reader's attention with clear, specific and concrete details.

168. The arch foe of clear phrasing is insincerity.

169. There are three absolute rules about dramatic order, but unfortunately no one knows what they are.

170. The arrangement of a story's elements is most successful when least noticed.

171. Structure cannot be imposed on a work, only evoked from within it.

172. Before starting, chart out a loose progression of the salient dramatic beats.

173. In terms of the painter's art, creative writing is self-portraiture.

174. A piece of writing will resonate when it's done. Fine-tune your sensibilities to feel when that moment arrives.

175. Anne Dillard said that every book presents two problems that a writer must solve: Can it be done? and, Can I do it?

176. A fine line separates the improbable from the impossible.

177. A writer with an understated style can make us believe most anything. Overstating can make us doubt the blue of the sky or the wet of the ocean.

178. Writing a story is like wrestling an octopus: Stick your hand in and turn the subject inside out.

179. Striking narrative is clear as the stare of a deer, as the dew on a rose, as the ringing of a hammer in the morning.

180. An author's style reflects an image of his soul. An author's technique is the fruit of hard work.

181. The only thing indispensable to a good style is personal sincerity.

182. Authentic, identifiable style is the writer's basic stuff made visible.

183. The more lucid and unaffected the prose, the more the stuff can shine through.

184. The biggest obstacle in capturing a personal style is the conscious attempt to affect one.

185. Style is the natural outcome of writing naturally.

186. The risk of a style with no burrs on it is that the work might pass through a reader's mind without leaving the slightest mark on it.

187. A windy style usually sounds like hot air.

188. Timeless work results only when a writer's style naturally fits his material.

189. In matters of style, modesty and common sense are sure guides.

190. Read your work out loud.

191. Language needs breathing room to have a life of its own.

192. Free the words and they come alive; control them too severely and you create a blueprint rather than a living organism.

193. Write about what amazes you and your words immediately take on high voltage.

194. A hunger to sound clever usually prevents a writer from becoming so.

195. A writer should always push for inspired expression.

196. Read the early stories of Jorge Luis Borges, which were tangled and laborious. Then read his final yarns, which were masterpieces of simplicity.

197. Overwriting typically comes from over thinking and under feeling.

198. Action refers to cannon blasts and transatlantic plane rides.

199. Movement refers to a chain of events involving desire, pursuit, conflict, crisis, etc., all leading to change in the character.

200. Characters discover things in crucial scenes, things leading to crux decisions, things that change lives. It's called movement.

201. A critical subtlety in any scene is the conflict between the way a character looks and the way he actually feels. Imparting this conflict without flagrant "telling" is high art.

202. When you want to say something, show it instead.

203. My favorite scenes are those in which an invisible sword, with a true and honed edge, is passed between characters. He who talks wields the sword. And everyone fears getting cut.

204. Pamela Douglass mentions the euphoria of flying with a scene rolling out like it's alive. "It's like an all-nighter when you can't get enough of each other, you and the characters, and no one wants to sleep ever again, and it's already there...just listen."

205. Aristotle said that *story* concerns the details that a reader needs to understand the plot.

206. Plot is the portion of the story that the writer presents--the dramatic beats of the narrative as they unfold in the present tense.

207. A "vision" of a story is a clear intuition grounded in a few dramatic beats or the light in a character's eyes.

208. A vision is the concrete emotional seed from which the live oak must grow. It is not the live oak itself, and it's frustrating and misguided to try and make it so.

209. You can never capture a vision on paper, but you should try to capture the understanding, which is the essence of craft, not intuition.

210. Everyone's life has unique facets that only the individual understands.

211. Trust that your uniqueness is your closest, most consequential material, and use it as the thin end of the wedge to open up your potential.

212. Insight is engaging, fine imagery agreeable, humor a balm; but only trouble is interesting.

213. Conflict, crisis and resolution remain the cornerstones of many great stories.

214. Only fairy tales are perfectly resolved. The most a solid story aims for is a fitting sense of completion.

215. The turning point in a "blockbuster" is reached only when a neutron bomb is set to go off. In real life, turning points are often furnished by seemingly minor events coming at just the right, or wrong, time.

216. Of the timeless themes (man against man; man against nature; man against machine; man against humanity; man against God), none grab me like the ultimate power struggle: man against himself.

217. "In devising a novel, it is perilous to start from an exciting theme. In general, a novel *about* something is always a disaster."

 – *James Michener*

218. Good fiction can enliven facts, but the reverse is not often true.

219. Attention is drawn toward a noble theme.

220. The theme is sustained through authenticity.

221. A story featuring clashing wills usually involves a power struggle.

222. A power struggle is only felt as one when the power changes hands several times.

223. Flop goes the story without a natural ending.

224. We need a sense that the ending is due.

225. It's fatal to introduce anything improbable late in your story.

226. Direct, personal experience is the bedrock of all writing. Personal experience, however, includes what is imagined.

227. Convincing stories are seldom "true."

228. Fiction is not based on fiction, rather it's imagining based on facts.

229. "Fiction is like a spider's web...attached to life at all four corners."
— *Virginia Wolfe*

230. A professional writer is a professional reviser.

231. If your most brutal editor isn't yourself, you're probably turning out dross.

232. Shrewd revising shortens the long and sharpens the general.

233. Think of revising in terms of an accordion: expanding and then contracting.

234. A sensitive writer can feel the intensity of individual scenes in his story or lines in his poem much like a Geiger counter can scan the terrain for uranium. Focus on dead spots.

235. Once a work has been painstakingly revised, it still requires buffing.

236. Before the final polish, let the work-- and yourself--simmer for a month or a year so you can gain new perspective.

237. Don't wait till you're done
      with a story to pass it around
      to friends and enemies.

238. Other eyes often spot weak, fuzzy and discrepant passages.

239. Search for where you have shown too much.

240. Develop the courage to trim sections that invariably are your favorites, but when measured against the whole, are dispensable.

241. It is torturous to prune writing you have slaved over--good reason to seek feedback before exhausting yourself over passages doomed to death.

242. The faulty thread is discovered only when the yarn has been spun all the way out.

243. Avoid the futility of exhausting yourself revising formative bits that will likely get dramatically retooled once a first draft is finished.

244. Original concepts change as a work discovers the one and only form in which it can survive.

245. The penalty for writing for someone other than myself is that I'll probably be the only person who has to read the disaster all the way through.

246. Second-guessing what the audience might fancy is creative suicide.

247. Identifying what we care about is often difficult.

248. Once school is over, many gifted people only pick up a book when they are tired, sick or lonely.

249. Curiosity brings two eyes to a book; interest keeps them on the page.

250. Reading is to the writer what roadwork is to the boxer.

251. Reading is the whetstone on which a writer hones his sword.

252. A classic story is a mirror in which many different readers see their reflections.

253. "A story is new to every reader because he himself recreates it."
    – *Jacob Bronowski*

254. In every great story I find
shards of my own biography.

255. A writer must read, and keep reading, to stay sharp and connected to the human race.

256. Some writers are so touchy that asking them how they feel about criticism is like asking a lamppost how it feels about dogs.

257. Once I became willing to do almost anything to improve my craft, criticism (some of it, anyway) became an asset rather than a right cross to my chin.

258. Only twice have I wanted to drag a critic 2,000 feet up El Capitan and lash him off to a rusty piton. Maybe three times.

259. Vicious criticism stings, but I've learned that if the critic hadn't taken me seriously, he wouldn't have put so much energy into the mugging.

260. My successful stories can't teach me much. My titanic failures have taught me volumes.

261. Most of my grievous mistakes came from following false assumptions.

262. Always believe that your readers are smarter than you are.

263. Asking a friend's opinion of your story is like a little girl asking her dad if she's pretty.

264. A steady diet of serious literature will ruin your appetite.

265. Most serious writers I know read tons of nonfiction, biographies, and "trash."

266. Eliot said that bad poets imitate, good poets steal.

267. It is said that stealing from one book is plagiarism; stealing from several books is research.

268. If writers weren't exquisite thieves, there'd be no great writing.

269. The only thing that makes a true story true is the inclusion of a physical incident that actually happened. Everything else is opinion.

270. The simplest mind can imagine a more beautiful woman or a handsomer man than the best writer can ever describe.

271. Writers who spend their time trying to discover what's true in their lives usually find something, and this something is almost always worth reading.

272. Whoever has known poverty, love and war has ten novels' worth of material.

273. William James said that true religion only starts when man looks up to the stars and says, "Help." Perhaps true writing doesn't begin till you put the plea to yourself.

274. Compulsive writing is a ritual of avoidance, and unless the author moves onto the ground he's running from, he's doomed to genre writing.

275. The few productive writers who are not consumed with sounding smart, with being thought of as geniuses--these are the few who are perfectly real. Their work has the heft of a mountain and the depth of the sea.

276. Frank Barron said the creative person "is more primitive and more cultivated, a lot madder and a lot saner than an average person."

277. When an author is committed to true and real things, he can hope for the sky, and occasionally reach it.

278. Hemingway said the most essential gift for a good writer "is a built-in shock-proof shit-detector."

279. A common saying is that the writer who expects results from a first novel is like the man who drops a rose petal into the Grand Canyon and listens for the echo.

280. Wanting to put an end to suffering is fundamental to all men. A writer never needs to justify such a quest.

281. A man on a street corner, a woman in a penthouse, a character in a book--they can all lie about love, money, deeds and fears. But no one ever lies about being lonely

282. It seems that half of contemporary film and literature is like taking a cruise through a sewer in a glass-bottom boat.

283. A touch of vulgar realism can effectively drive home a point; but while most readers will follow you to the outhouse, few want to be locked inside.

284. "Working upon the vulgar with fine sense is like attempting to hew blocks with a razor."

– Pope

285. Humor is the most difficult magic because it's not about funny words, which anyone can string together.

286. First comes the tragically absurd
      situation, where laughing and crying
      are much the same thing. Next comes
      comic situations, and a dozen rungs
      below that, wit. The bottom rungs are
      gags and wisecracking.

287. Wit is not a kind of jam you can spread
      on a story.

288. Clear and permanent solutions are achieved by Zen masters, not characters in a story.

289. Shrewd thematic arrangement can enhance, but never displace, the need for vitality and humanity in the narrated action.

290. A mediocre writer can arrange thoughts but a magnificent writer cannot reshuffle and fine-tune emotions.

291. Emotions emerge jumbled and intertwined with love and anger and pain and desire, and should be left that way.

292. No writer is good enough to manufacture meaning if it isn't inherently there.

293. Avoid talking in proverbs or you might say things like, "No leg is too short to reach the ground."

294. If you don't consecrate your work with honesty, readers will follow your lead and dismiss you as insignificant.

295. Without suffering, soul-searching and wrestling with God, many writers can't get to the bottom of anything.

296. Ultimately, no writer can work authentically under a set of rules, or extrude his work through prevailing tastes.

297. You read all you can bear to read, learn what you can, realize it at the cellular level and work from instinct.

298. There is not a person who has lived forty years who couldn't write a lasting novel if only they knew how to shift the gravity of their memories onto the empty pages.

299. Have courage. Let the writing travel into unknown waters.

300. What a colossal act of ego it is to work alone, week after week, in the expectation others may care to read what you've written. Thank God for your ego.

301.   The doctor says you have two years to live, just enough time to figure out and complete the only book that means anything to you. Do you need the doctor's prognosis to get cracking?

302. Every writer stands on a creaky pier and throws his net out to sea. Into waters never dreamed of, the net drifts. Hands bleed hauling it in. The heart hopes after excellence, fortune, fame; but the inmost desire is to net ourselves.